STATE PROFILES

MISSISSIPPI

BY COLLEEN SEXTON

BELLWETHER MEDIA • MINNEAPOLIS, MN

Blastoff! Discovery launches a new mission: reading to learn. Filled with facts and features, each book offers you an exciting new world to explore!

BLASTOFF! UNIVERSE

BLASTOFF! Beginners — GRADE K

BLASTOFF! READERS — GRADES 1-3

BLASTOFF! DISCOVERY — GRADE 4

This edition first published in 2022 by Bellwether Media, Inc.

No part of this publication may be reproduced in whole or in part without written permission of the publisher.
For information regarding permission, write to Bellwether Media, Inc.,
Attention: Permissions Department,
6012 Blue Circle Drive, Minnetonka, MN 55343.

Library of Congress Cataloging-in-Publication Data

Names: Sexton, Colleen A., 1967- author.
Title: Mississippi / by Colleen Sexton.
Description: Minneapolis, MN : Bellwether Media, Inc., 2022. |
    Series: Blastoff! Discovery: State profiles | Includes bibliographical
    references and index. | Audience: Ages 7-13 | Audience: Grades
    4-6 | Summary: "Engaging images accompany information about
    Mississippi. The combination of high-interest subject matter and
    narrative text is intended for students in grades 3 through 8"–
    Provided by publisher.
Identifiers: LCCN 2021019679 (print) | LCCN 2021019680 (ebook)
    | ISBN 9781644873953 (library binding) | ISBN
    9781648341724 (ebook)
Subjects: LCSH: Mississippi–Juvenile literature.
Classification: LCC F341.3 .S49 2022 (print) | LCC F341.3 (ebook)
    | DDC 976.2–dc23
LC record available at https://lccn.loc.gov/2021019679
LC ebook record available at https://lccn.loc.gov/2021019680

Editor: Rebecca Sabelko   Designer: Kathleen Petelinsek

Printed in the United States of America, North Mankato, MN.

TABLE OF CONTENTS

CYPRESS SWAMP
NATCHEZ TRACE PARKWAY

Time to hit the road! A family is driving the Natchez Trace Parkway through Mississippi. The long road winds through a thick forest. The family stops to hike in Cypress Swamp. Tall tupelo and bald cypress trees surround them as they follow a boardwalk trail over water.

OTHER TOP SITES

DELTA BLUES MUSEUM

GULF ISLANDS NATIONAL SEASHORE

MISSISSIPPI CIVIL RIGHTS MUSEUM

VICKSBURG NATIONAL MILITARY PARK

More driving leads to the French Camp Historic Village. The family learns how early **settlers** lived. They also visit the Pharr Mounds. Early hunters and gatherers built these earthen mounds. The family's last stop is Tishomingo State Park. They set up camp for the night and enjoy their beautiful surroundings. Welcome to Mississippi!

5

Mississippi is in the southeastern United States. This tall, narrow state covers 48,432 square miles (125,438 square kilometers). Arkansas and Louisiana lie across the Mississippi River along Mississippi's western border. Tennessee lies to the north. Alabama is Mississippi's eastern neighbor. The waters of the **Gulf** of Mexico meet Mississippi's short southern border. The Mississippi **Sound** separates a string of **barrier islands** from the **mainland**.

Jackson is the capital and largest city. It is located near the center of the state. Other major cities include Gulfport, Southaven, Biloxi, and Hattiesburg.

TENNESSEE

SOUTHAVEN

ARKANSAS

MISSISSIPPI
RIVER

MISSISSIPPI

LOUISIANA

★ JACKSON

ALABAMA

HATTIESBURG

GULFPORT   BILOXI

7

GULF OF MEXICO

VICKSBURG NATIONAL
MILITARY PARK
CIVIL WAR BATTLEFIELD

People first arrived in Mississippi about 12,000 years ago. Over time, Native American groups formed. The Choctaw were farmers and traders. They lived in southern and central Mississippi. The Natchez grew crops in the southwest. The Chickasaw lived in villages in the northeast.

THE TRAIL OF TEARS

In the 1830s, the U.S. government forced the Choctaw and Chickasaw tribes in Mississippi to move west to Oklahoma. Thousands died during this long journey known as the Trail of Tears.

Europeans first explored Mississippi in the 1500s. Settlers established cotton **plantations**. Many **enslaved** Africans labored on these large farms. By the late 1700s, the United States controlled the region. Mississippi became the 20th state in 1817. The state fought for the South in the **Civil War** from 1861 to 1865.

NATIVE PEOPLES OF MISSISSIPPI

MISSISSIPPI BAND OF CHOCTAW INDIANS

- Original lands in Mississippi and western Alabama
- Around 10,000 members in Mississippi today
- Also called Chahta

CHOCTAW PLAYING A GAME

Western Mississippi's **Delta** region is full of rich soil. It was spread over thousands of years by flooding along the Mississippi River. **Bayous** flow through wetlands along the Mississippi River and near the coast. **Plains** cover the rest of the state. The **Black Belt** in the northeast supports crops and livestock. The thick forests of the Piney Woods rise in the southeast. Sandy shores stretch along the coast.

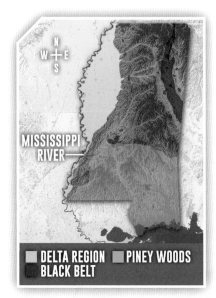

MISSISSIPPI RIVER

◻ DELTA REGION   ◻ PINEY WOODS
◼ BLACK BELT

MISSISSIPPI BAYOU

NAME DROPPING

Mississippi takes its name from the Mississippi River. The river is more than 2,300 miles (3,701 kilometers) long! It begins in Minnesota and flows to the Gulf of Mexico.

SPRING
HIGH: 75°F (24°C)
LOW: 51°F (11°C)

SUMMER
HIGH: 91°F (33°C)
LOW: 69°F (21°C)

FALL
HIGH: 76°F (24°C)
LOW: 52°F (11°C)

WINTER
HIGH: 57°F (14°C)
LOW: 35°F (2°C)

°F = degrees Fahrenheit
°C = degrees Celsius

BILOXI BEACH AFTER HURRICANE KATRINA

MISSISSIPPI'S FUTURE: HURRICANE WARNING

Scientists predict more powerful hurricanes due to climate change. Winds will be stronger. There will be more rain. Mississippi's government urges residents to be prepared. They should keep emergency supplies on hand and follow plans to move inland.

Mississippi's winters are mild. Hot, muggy summers often bring severe weather. Thunderstorms and tornadoes sweep across the state. **Hurricanes** blow in from the Gulf of Mexico. They threaten the coast in summer and fall.

11

NINE-BANDED ARMADILLO

Mississippi's fields, forests, and waters are full of life. Deer munch on grasses in fields. Foxes leave their dens to hunt rabbits and mice. Copperhead snakes slither along the forest floor. Armadillos dig near streams, while bald eagles soar overhead. Wild turkeys peck the ground for seeds and insects. They roost in trees as night falls. The songs of mockingbirds fill the evening air.

WILD TURKEY

Alligators and cottonmouth snakes glide through swamps. Bass, catfish, and crappies swim in the state's lakes and rivers. Coastal waters are home to whales and dolphins. Crabs, oysters, and shrimp live there, too.

AMERICAN ALLIGATOR

COMMON BOTTLENOSE DOLPHIN

BALD EAGLE

WHITE-TAILED DEER

Life Span: around 2 to 3 years
Status: least concern

white-tailed deer =

LEAST CONCERN	NEAR THREATENED	VULNERABLE	ENDANGERED	CRITICALLY ENDANGERED	EXTINCT IN THE WILD	EXTINCT

About 3 million people live in Mississippi. Around half of all Mississippians live on farms and in small towns. Others live in cities and surrounding areas. They include the Gulfport-Biloxi-Pascagoula area, Hattiesburg, and Jackson.

FARM IN MISSISSIPPI

MISSISSIPPI'S CHALLENGE: DECREASING POPULATION

The population of Mississippi is decreasing. People are leaving for jobs in other states. Fewer people are left in Mississippi to pay taxes. There is less money for government services. Lawmakers must pass laws to bring workers back.

GULFPORT

Mississippi's rich farmland drew many **immigrants** in the late 1700s. They came from England, Ireland, and Germany. Many of their **descendants** live in Mississippi today. About two of every five Mississippians are African American or Black. Small numbers of people with Asian, Hispanic, and Native American backgrounds call the state home. Recent immigrants come from Mexico, Guatemala, India, the Philippines, and Vietnam.

In 1792, LeFleur's **Bluff** became a trading post on the Pearl River in Mississippi. This site was named Jackson in 1821. It became Mississippi's capital in 1822. Today, Jackson is the state's largest city and center of industry.

A CAPITAL NAME

Mississippi's capital was named for Andrew Jackson. He was a hero of the War of 1812 and later became president of the United States.

Jackson's residents enjoy a rich **culture**. Many attend performances by the symphony, opera, and ballet. Visitors to the Mississippi **Civil Rights** Museum learn about African Americans' struggle for human rights. The Museum of Natural Science and Mississippi Museum of Art draw curious crowds. The Fondren neighborhood is famous for its shops and restaurants. LeFleur's Bluff State Park is a great spot for outdoor fun.

MISSISSIPPI CIVIL RIGHTS MUSEUM

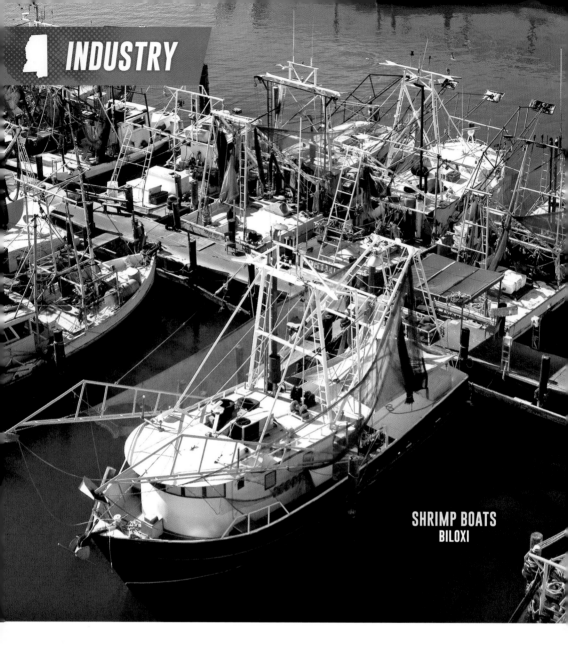

SHRIMP BOATS
BILOXI

Mississippi's rich soil drives the state's farming industry. Corn, cotton, soybeans, rice, and sweet potatoes grow on small farms throughout the state. Farmers also raise young chickens for their meat. Shrimp from Gulf waters is packaged in coastal factories. Workers drill for oil and natural gas in southern Mississippi.

Some Mississippians build cars and ships. At the Stennis Space Center, workers test rocket engines. Most Mississippians have **service jobs**. They work in banks, hospitals, and schools. Some serve visitors in hotels and restaurants.

STENNIS SPACE CENTER

INVENTED IN MISSISSIPPI

BARQ'S ROOT BEER

Date Invented: 1898
Inventor: Edward C. Barq

PINE-SOL

Date Invented: 1929
Inventor: Harry Cole

HUMAN LUNG TRANSPLANT

Date Invented: 1963
Inventors: James D. Hardy and team, University of Mississippi Medical Center

TAMALES

Meals bring Mississippians together. Barbecue is a favorite. Pork is slow cooked with seasonings and sauces. On the side, cooks add collard greens and mashed potatoes with gravy. Mississippians often cook up catfish, okra, and sweet potatoes.

TASTY TAMALES

Mexicans brought tamales to Mississippi more than 100 years ago. Tamales are corn dough filled with meat. They are cooked in a corn husk. Street vendors and restaurants throughout the Delta offer this tasty dish.

Seafood boils are fun events. Crawfish, corn, and potatoes fill large pots. This meal is dumped out on a table for everyone to dig in and enjoy. The feast is washed down with a cold glass of sweet tea. Mississippi mud pie, pecan pie, and blackberry cobbler are favorite desserts.

SEAFOOD BOIL

MISSISSIPPI MUD PIE

8 SERVINGS

Have an adult help you make this mud pie!

INGREDIENTS

1 9-inch baked pie crust

1/2 cup (1 stick) butter, melted

1 3/4 cups sugar

4 tablespoons cocoa

1/4 cup all-purpose flour

4 eggs, beaten

1 teaspoon vanilla extract

3 cups vanilla ice cream, softened

3 tablespoons fudge sauce

DIRECTIONS

1. Preheat the oven to 350 degrees Fahrenheit (177 degrees Celsius).
2. In a bowl, stir together the butter, sugar, and cocoa until well combined.
3. Add the flour, eggs, and vanilla. Mix until smooth.
4. Pour the mixture into the crust.
5. Bake for 30 to 40 minutes. Remove the pie from the oven and cool completely.
6. Gently mound ice cream on the pie. Freeze until the ice cream sets.
7. Drizzle the pie with fudge sauce before serving.

Mississippi offers great outdoor adventures. Kayakers paddle the state's rivers and lakes. Fishers pull in bass, crappies, and catfish. Hikers and campers enjoy the state's vast forests. Trails for bicycling and horseback riding are a big draw. The sandy beaches along the Gulf invite swimmers and snorkelers. Mississippians also enjoy exploring the state's many art galleries, museums, and historic sites.

Football is the most popular sport in Mississippi. The state does not have any professional teams. But fans fill the stands to cheer on the Ole Miss Rebels and the Mississippi State Bulldogs.

MISSISSIPPI STATE BULLDOG FANS

NOTABLE SPORTS TEAM

Ole Miss Rebels, University of Mississippi
Sport: National Collegiate Athletic Association football
Started: 1893
Place of Play: Vaught-Hemingway Stadium

23

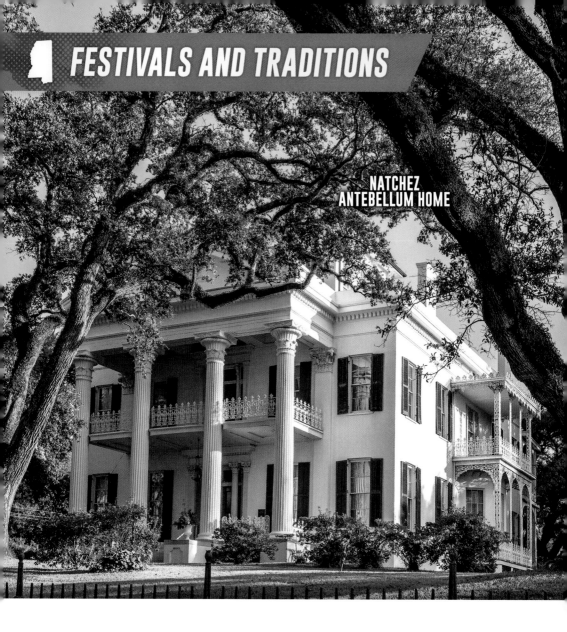

FESTIVALS AND TRADITIONS

NATCHEZ
ANTEBELLUM HOME

Mississippi's festivals celebrate the state's culture. In spring and fall, **antebellum** mansions open their doors for the Natchez **Pilgrimage**. Costumed guides tell visitors about these homes and the people who lived there. Biloxi marks the beginning of the shrimping season each June with the Blessing of the Fleet. This event also features seafood, artists, and entertainment.

24

Blues music has deep roots in the state. The Mississippi Delta Blues Festival in Greenville honors the music each September. In October, more than 600,000 people attend the Mississippi State Fair. Free musical performances, livestock shows, and more entertain fairgoers. Fun festivals bring Mississippians together!

SINGING THE BLUES

Blues music dates to the 1800s. Enslaved peoples chanted along with the rhythm of their work in the fields. These chants mixed with folk music and religious songs called spirituals to create the blues style.

MISSISSIPPI STATE FAIR

1541

Hernando de Soto of Spain is likely the first European to pass through the Mississippi region

1861

Mississippi leaves the United States and joins the Confederate States of America

1817

Mississippi becomes the 20th U.S. state

1798

The United States gains control of the area that is now Mississippi

1830s

The U.S. government forces the Choctaw and Chickasaw tribes of Mississippi to move west of the Mississippi River

2005

Hurricane Katrina strikes the Gulf Coast, taking the lives of more than 200 Mississippians and destroying many homes and businesses

2018

Cindy Hyde-Smith becomes the first woman from Mississippi elected to the U.S. Congress

1969

The U.S. Supreme Court orders Mississippi's schools to desegregate so that Black students and white students no longer attend separate schools

1927

Barriers along the Mississippi River break after heavy rains, leading to the Great Flood of 1927

2021

Mississippi replaces its state flag with a new design that does not display any Confederate symbols

Nickname: The Magnolia State

State Motto: *Virtute et Armis* (By Valor and Arms)

Date of Statehood: December 10, 1817
(the 20th state)

Capital City: Jackson ★

Other Major Cities: Gulfport, Southaven, Biloxi, Hattiesburg

Area: 48,432 square miles (125,438 square kilometers); Mississippi is the 32nd largest state.

Population

2,961,279
(2020)

STATE FLAG

Mississippi adopted its state flag in 2021. It features a magnolia blossom, the state flower, on a blue background. Vertical bands of red and gold are on either side. Twenty white stars circle the blossom, showing that Mississippi is the 20th state. A gold star at the top represents the state's Native American people. The flag also includes the U.S. motto, "In God We Trust."

INDUSTRY

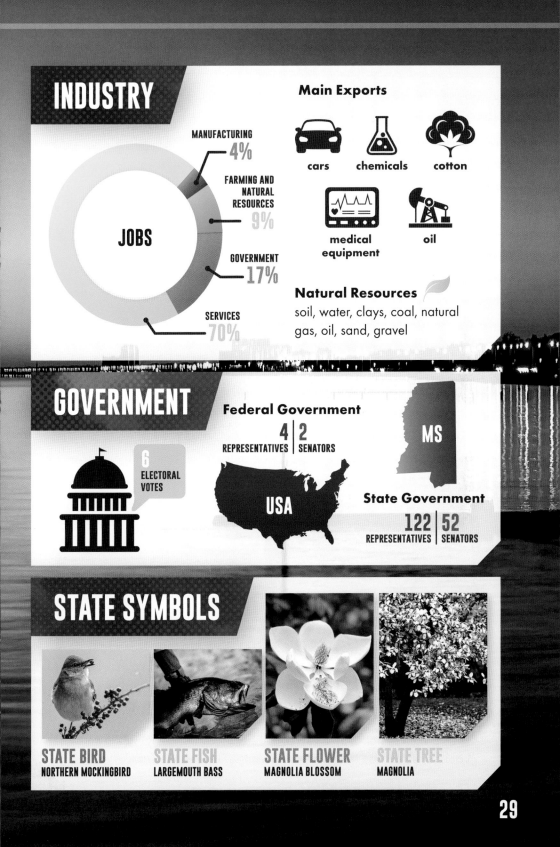

JOBS

MANUFACTURING
4%

FARMING AND NATURAL RESOURCES
9%

GOVERNMENT
17%

SERVICES
70%

Main Exports

cars

chemicals

cotton

medical equipment

oil

Natural Resources

soil, water, clays, coal, natural gas, oil, sand, gravel

GOVERNMENT

Federal Government

4 REPRESENTATIVES | **2** SENATORS

6 ELECTORAL VOTES

USA

MS

State Government

122 REPRESENTATIVES | **52** SENATORS

STATE SYMBOLS

STATE BIRD
NORTHERN MOCKINGBIRD

STATE FISH
LARGEMOUTH BASS

STATE FLOWER
MAGNOLIA BLOSSOM

STATE TREE
MAGNOLIA

antebellum—related to the period before the Civil War

barrier islands—long, sandy islands along a shore created by wind and waves

bayous—slow-moving streams of water in marshy areas

Black Belt—a strip of rich farmland in Alabama and Mississippi known for growing cotton

bluff—a cliff or steep bank that often overlooks a body of water

civil rights—the rights of citizens to freedom and equality

Civil War—a war between the Northern (Union) and Southern (Confederate) states that lasted from 1861 to 1865

culture—the beliefs, arts, and ways of life in a place or society

delta—a land area that forms where a river flows into a large body of water

descendants—relatives of people who lived long ago

enslaved—to be considered property and forced to work for no pay

gulf—part of an ocean or sea that extends into land

hurricanes—storms formed in the tropics that have violent winds and often have rain and lightning

immigrants—people who move to a new country

mainland—a continent or main part of a continent

pilgrimage—a long journey

plains—large areas of flat land

plantations—large farms that grow coffee beans, cotton, rubber, or other crops; plantations are mainly found in warm climates.

service jobs—jobs that perform tasks for people or businesses

settlers—people who move to live in a new, undeveloped region

sound—a long waterway separating a mainland and an island or connecting two larger bodies of water

TO LEARN MORE

AT THE LIBRARY

Gagliardi, Sue. *Hurricane Katrina*. Lake Elmo, Minn.: Focus Readers, 2020.

Rodger, Ellen. *Mississippi River Research Journal*. New York, N.Y.: Crabtree Publishing, 2018.

Zeiger, Jennifer. *Mississippi*. New York, N.Y.: Children's Press, 2018.

ON THE WEB

FACTSURFER

Factsurfer.com gives you a safe, fun way to find more information.

1. Go to www.factsurfer.com.

2. Enter "Mississippi" into the search box and click Q.

3. Select your book cover to see a list of related content.

INDEX